Why Yes to God: Essays on Life and God by College-Age Adults.

© 2013 by Nina M. Thompson, NICHE
Public Relations and Communications
nicheprandcomm@yahoo.com
http://www.nicheprandcomm.com

ALL RIGHTS RESERVED. This book
contains material protected under
International and Federal Copyright Laws
and Treaties. Any unauthorized reprint or
use of this material is prohibited. No part of
this book may be reproduced or transmitted
in any form or by any means, electronic or
mechanical, including photocopying,
recording, or by any information storage and
retrieval system without express written
permission from the author.

Published by Rycraw Productions
Creve Coeur, Mo 63141

ISBN: 978-0-9910287-0-2
Printed in the United States

FOREWORD
by Nina Thompson

The fact that you picked up this book with the title, "Why Yes to God: Essays on life and God by young adults," speaks volumes. It demonstrates that you are searching for a better way to live your life; a way that will alleviate some of the pain, some of the loneliness, and some of the emptiness that life can often deposit within us.

It demonstrates that you are in need of a more promising future, more mutually beneficial and spiritually uplifting relationships, and basically, more peace and joy. It also shows me that you are looking for something that will yield a better way to deal with the negative influences in your life, the constant battles, fights and arguments, the tension, the aching that never seems to subside and the emptiness.

The fact that you picked up this book also indicates that you are ready to say "yes" to something greater and more fulfilling than you have ever had in your life. Though you may not know it yet, you want to say "yes" to purpose and you want to associate with others who are on their way to doing that.

Now, you may not know exactly what that purpose is or even that the "something" you are looking for falls in line with your purpose. You may not even know what you should say "yes" to exactly. Maybe it's that opportunity to go back to school and obtain your degree. Maybe it's that job offer in another state that would let you start over again. Maybe it's the young man or woman whom you met at the party last night that could make your life what it needs to be. Maybe all of that and then some might be just the things to 'fix' your life and set it on track. Maybe – but experience teaches that all of those things pass away and you are still left with who you are, your same desires to be something better, and your need to understand why you are here.

If you choose not to explore your greater purpose now, without any apparent reason, one day you may wake up and wonder why you are still dating "that person," working at "that job," or indulging in "that negative habit." One day you may wake up and realize that none of those were your "yes" and just maybe your "yes" was a force that was vastly greater than anything that you could touch or feel. Maybe it was something with the power to guide, direct and lead you into the fulfillment of your true purpose in this life; something greater than you or I.

For billions of people just like you, between the ages of 18 and 25, that "yes" has turned out to be a relationship with God. Opening minds, eyes, ears and entire bodies to God has helped countless young people find purpose, peace and productivity within their lives. The simple step of allowing God to lead, guide and direct their way, while birthing the God-given gifts, talents and abilities that have been placed within them, provides them with an extraordinary journey. It is the best decision that many people have ever made, and I suggest that it will be the best one that you will ever make.

Let the words of the young leaders within these pages guide you. As you read their essays, share in their experiences with God, church, family, friends and life challenges, you will gain greater understanding of what "yes" is and means. As they take you on their journey to move toward oneness with God and activation of their spiritual gifts and talents, see the possibilities that a move like this can offer to you in your life. You will learn that it is more than attending church, wearing the right clothes, doing all the right things and being nice to others.

I encourage you to spend time thinking and responding to the questions at the end of the essays. Keep a diary while you are going through the process and date each page. This will help you to document how God is working within your life and helping to lead you to purpose, peace and productivity. If you work through these questions, they will cause you to think, reflect and reevaluate your past experiences with church and God to a more positive and gratifying end.

You always have a choice. You can choose to keep living the same dull, stale, dangerous, empty and unfulfilled life, or you can strike out in another direction and say "yes" to something better, something greater, something powerful. Think about it.

*What if Noah had said "no" to building the ark? Would you exist today?

*What if the disciple Paul or any disciple had said "no" to connecting people to God? Just read your Bible and remove all that they accomplished and all that they teach us.

*What if Mary, mother of Jesus, had said "no." Not only did she say yes, she gave a beautiful response. "My soul magnifies the Lord."

*What if Jesus had said, "No.?"

Table of Contents

Pastor's Message

In 1Timothy chapter 4, Paul admonishes Timothy not to let anyone look down upon him because of his youth, but to set an example for the believers in speech, in conduct, in love, in faith, and in purity. This collection of essays is such an example of modern-day Timothy's and Tameka's and their on-going journey to say "Yes to God!"

Like Timothy, I have assisted the lead pastor. I have been the mentee, the trainee-in-ministry, gopher, and new pastor at a hellish church. The Holy Spirit and ministry make me humble with memories of those times.

Now serving in a role more likened to Paul; church planter, mentor, teacher, parent and more, I recognize my "Timothy" experiences have shaped my present spiritual practices, pastoral vision and personal affinity for discipleship of youth and young adults.

Since its inception Wellspring Church has intentionally welcomed persons of varied backgrounds, diverse experiences, ages, orientations, professional dispositions and spiritual understanding. Respectfully, our church has responded to the challenge and charge to grow an intergenerational learning and teaching community.

Wellspring exists to reach persons, to connect them with other Christians, to help them grow their faith and to offer themselves in service, in order to celebrate God with their life. Our congregation is blessed to a have a college-age minister, Nina Thompson, whose heart, spiritual gifts, and professional experiences undergird this ministerial call. As pastor, I have witnessed young men and women grow from spectators to participants. Over time many have transitioned from mere visitor to vested and willing vessels for the Lord. Truth is some have even emerged from their sleeping during sermons to preparing their own initial sermon. Thanks to God for this vital and fruitful ministry

model.

Essays On Going to Church

Essay One

I didn't even think about going to church during this part of my life because I left for college. I knew that every church could treat you differently, but I wasn't ready for what I might find.

Before I went off to college, I joined a nice, friendly church. Everyone embraced me and showed me unconditional love (so I thought). While I was there, I learned a lot about God and how to pray and enter into his presence. Then near graduation time, things started to get a little different, but they were still nice and giving me gifts. Finally, when it was time for me to leave they told me that we could have live chats during prayer services and they even prayed for me before I left.

The first time I went back home everyone embraced me and gave me words of encouragement before I left, but when I returned again after a few months at school, it was like I was the devil himself when I walked into the church. They made me feel like I was wrong for going away to college: I felt like as long as I was attending school "out there" I wasn't good enough to be a part of their church. I asked myself, "where are the hugs, the words of encouragement, the same people that just told me they loved me like a sister?

It may have been that I just didn't fit anymore.

I stopped attending church for a while after that because I didn't like that feeling. I felt like everybody was more advanced than me; that I wasn't holy enough to worship with them.

There was one lady that never treated me that way though. She was always there if I needed to talk. She even encouraged me to begin my own prayer group while I was away at school and I did it. The girls in my dorm loved it, because they wanted that same connection with God that I did.

One day while I was in town, she called me and said "You should come visit my church. " My sister talked about it all the time, so I said "let me go see."

It was great. I loved the preached word and the lady was very happy to see me and I was happy to see her.

After I returned home from school for good, I just kept visiting the church since I lived in the area. One day the lady came up to me and my sister and said you all should come to our "Yes to God" (YTG) meetings. I didn't know what that was, but I was willing to follow her "till the wheels fell off" because I knew she was a true woman of God.

I attended one class and I didn't know what to think. I walked into the class like a "miss know it all" with my bible like I was going to teach them something. Little did I know that they were teaching classes, giving prophetic words to each other and conducting a whole lot of other Holy-spirit led-activities.

I thought this was amazing because they were just like me. One girl even told me that at first she thought I was the "I sleep with my bible type of girl."

Meeting them and coming to YTG is what has really kept me running to God. Now I know when God is speaking to me and I can give prophetic words to people that God directs me to speak to. I thank God for that lady (If she reads this she will know she is the one). If it wasn't for her, I don't think I would have ever found a great new church home or discovered the gifts that God has placed within me.

Essay Two

I didn't ever feel like church was a safe zone for me; that's why I didn't want to join.

I felt as if I would be judged, and I would not feel comfortable. I just felt like I would not fit in and it just was not the place for me.

Growing up I was taught that we had to go to church every Sunday, and I did not understand why I had to go to listen to people that I did not understand teach me about a Bible that I didn't understand, in order to be a child of God; in order to be saved?

I had a lot of questions, too. If this is the house of the Lord, then why can't I feel comfortable? Do I have to go to church to go to heaven? I had so many questions with no answers, so I stayed away.

I thought that I would rather go to the club, where I fit in, where I wasn't judged, and where there are other people just like me…lost.

Something in my heart always had a passion for God no matter where I was or what I was doing. He has always been on my mind, in my heart and in my spirit. So, eventually, I could not resist it anymore. I responded to a request from my friend to come to church, and then joined the YTG group, and I haven't looked back. I am working in my spiritual gifts and enjoying my journey with God. I also have brought a lot of others into the YTG group as well.

Essay Three

I did not like church and never thought that I would ever go back because as a child, my mother forced my sisters and I to go. We use to be there all day. I was a kid and I didn't even know what this man was talking about. I just knew he just wouldn't stop talking. I was happy when I found out that they were starting a children's church; I lit up like a Christmas tree when I was told.

As I got older I saw people start to leave the church and then new people came. Other people started talking about them. My mother eventually took us out of that church, but by this time I was a teenager and was trying to "kick it." I wasn't worried about that place called "church." I use to spend the night at my friend's house just so I wouldn't have to go. When my friends and I started to praise dance and we came up with a name for our dance team, we were then inspired to attend church again.

There were 6-8 girls in the group, but we all grew up. Some had kids. Others went to college, but, I fell madly in love with another female. I would do anything for her. I fought my family and didn't care what people thought or had to say. When we moved in together, all Hell broke loose. I was cheating on her, she was cheating on me. We started fighting a lot. She started lying about the smallest things. I knew that it was time for us to move on. I ended up moving away with a family member.

Though the girl and I were still talking, I started talking to this guy I worked with. He was very sweet to me and gave me everything I wanted. He felt so perfect and it felt so right to be with him until I found I was pregnant. He couldn't deal with it at all and wanted me to abort "it" as if we didn't make this baby together. Long story short, no baby and no him.

I had hit rock bottom and I was under the "rock," until I talked to my best friend and she took me to a church. It was very small but it was cool because everyone in there was my age or a little older. I thought that I had found a new home. People were so nice and everybody was friendly. I was even on the praise dance team.

One day, though, people started leaving the church again. They started asking us to do things that I had never heard of and people started acting differently. So, I slowly started pushing my way out of the church. I didn't show up for some of the meetings or classes and really wasn't there on Sundays. One day I really wanted to go to church because I had a very bad week, but I didn't have any gas in my car. I ended up going to a church right down the street from my house.

When I say "we had church that day," we had it. I walked out of that church and felt like a new person. I felt like I could smile again, I could be myself again, and not have to worry about anything.

Now I'm in a college-age ministry group called "Yes to God" and I love it. They made me feel important, taught me that there are other people going through rough times. They taught me to pray always. I learned that if you feel like you can't do anything else, you should just pray.

Essay Four

I didn't want to attend church at first because I didn't really see anybody at the church that was my age and people who had gone to church before made it seem like we had to do it; just because "it was the right thing to do." They never really cared if I believed in God or not; they just wanted to see people coming to church. Now, I can't say that this is true of all churches, but I think it is true of most of them.

Another reason why I didn't want to attend church was because I never had anyone to really explain to me what church really was and to really teach me about God. They never took time to help me understand who God was and why God put us on Earth, but I always believed in God.

Finally, I thought that if I didn't give money, I wasn't doing the right thing, but most of that has changed now. I joined YTG and then I joined Wellspring Church this year on my own. No one forced me to walk to the altar. No one threatened me with going to Hell. I made a choice and I don't regret it.

SELF EXPLORATION: Please answer honestly and thoughtfully.

1. Which essay related to church attendance seems to hit closer to your feelings about church? Are there several? Explain.

_____

_____

_____

_____

_____

_____

_____

_____

_____

_____

_____

_____

_____

_____

_____

_____

_____

_____

_____

_____

_____

_____

_____

2. Have you ever sat in church without a clue as to what was being preached or discussed? How did that make you feel? How could you become more engaged in helping yourself to better understand?

_____

_____

_____

_____

_____

_____

_____

_____

_____

_____

_____

_____

_____

_____

_____

_____

_____

_____

_____

3. Do you feel pressure to "fit in" or be a certain way (dress, hair, speech, etc.) in order to be accepted by other church attendees? Have you ever felt out of place in a church or place of worship? Describe your emotions. What did you do? How would you help others work through these feelings?

_____

_____

_____

_____

_____

_____

_____

_____

_____

_____

_____

_____

_____

_____

_____

_____

_____

_____

_____

_____

_____

_____

_____

_____

Scriptures for further study:
<u>Church attendance</u>:
Hebrews 10:25, Romans 12:5, 1
Corinthians 12:27
<u>Judging Others</u>:
Luke 6:37, John 7:24, Matthew 7:1-5

Essays on What God Feels Like
Essay One

I was confused about God during the majority of my childhood. I grew up a Christian, going to church with my mom, and hating getting up early to go. I listened though and I tried my best to understand, but I didn't understand.

The confusion really came when my dad tried to teach me about the Muslim religion. I am not one of those Christians who will "put down" other religions, but I choose to be a Christian and my beliefs do not align with the Muslim religion. My dad totally confused me, not saying he was teaching me bad things, but he made me confused about what beliefs went with what religion. I was very young and curious about a ton of things. I had gotten so confused and curious; I even went as far as studying all religions, even Satanism.

I shortly became extremely depressed and even tried to commit suicide at 17. That is also when I renewed my faith in Jesus Christ.

Everyone was stunned by my new behaviors and beliefs! I was a new person! I was confident and I loved myself! This was my start of speaking into people's lives as a prophetess, and it was life changing. God started to use me in so many ways!

I have a gift of dreaming and God is able to speak to me in dreams. I am able to warn other people of what's to come, however, some people's reactions are not so welcoming sometimes. Some claimed I was a physic or did the devil's work, but they're wrong!

A lot of people don't understand that God puts gifts in all of us! Not everyone is capable of doing the same thing or even at the same level, but God put something special in all of us! The question is, how do you tap into that gift? "Yes to God" has helped me tap into my gift in levels I'd never imagined! I am only 20 now so just imagine if I keep myself aligned with God's will where will I be? Only God knows, and I cannot wait for God to move me and use me. So what are you waiting for? God has gifts just for you with your name on it! Now own them!

SELF EXPLORATION: Please answer honestly and thoughtfully.

1. Examine and express your feelings about confusion related to different religions and denominations. What can you do to avoid this type of confusion?

_____

_____

_____

_____

_____

_____

_____

_____

_____

_____

_____

_____

_____

_____

_____

_____

_____

_____

_____

_____

_____

_____

_____

2. Have you ever considered suicide?
   Why? Do you think a strong
   relationship with God and
   understanding your spiritual gifts
   could have helped you through this
   troubled time? Explain.

_____

_____

_____

_____

_____

_____

_____

_____

_____

_____

_____

_____

_____

_____

_____

_____

_____

_____

_____

_____

3. How did the author's discovery of
   spiritual gifts that God has given and
   expression about those gifts make
   you feel? Do you think it would be a
   positive experience or is this
   something that is strange for you to
   think about? Why?

_____

_____

_____

_____

_____

_____

_____

_____

_____

_____

_____

_____

_____

_____

_____

_____

_____

_____

_____

Essay Two

The first time that I felt that God actually could have called me to be both a prophet and a preacher, I was shocked. I kept thinking to myself, "God has given me these gifts that allow me to tell people what God tells me to share with them, words that lift them up, and to spread the Word of God." I thought of what a blessing that was.

Sometimes I just can't believe it and then I start to question it. What if I'm not really hearing from God? What if I am only saying just what's on my own mind and not the right things? What if people don't "feel" what I am saying? This is what I said before.

Now, I truly believe that God has given me this gift and I am going to use it and spread it as far and wide as God dictates. It is a lot or work, but I am ready.

SELF EXPLORATION: Please answer honestly and thoughtfully.

1. Do you think that finding your God-given destiny is tied to discovering your overall life's destiny? Why or why not?

_____

_____

_____

_____

_____

_____

_____

_____

_____

_____

_____

_____

_____

_____

_____

_____

_____

_____

2. Do you believe that God has given each person spiritual gifts, talents and abilities? Do you believe that God speaks to and through us? If so, write down an experience you have had with hearing from God.

_____

_____

_____

_____

_____

3. Do you know your spiritual gifts,
    talents and abilities? If not, do you
    know where to go for help to
    discover them? Would you be afraid
    to use them?

_____

_____

_____

_____

_____

_____

_____

_____

_____

_____

_____

_____

_____

_____

_____

_____

_____

Scriptures for further study:
Spiritual Gifts: Romans 12:6-8, 1 Peter
4:10-11, Ephesians 4:11-16, 1 Corinthians
12:27-28

Essays on Saying "Yes"

Essay One

To describe what it feels like to finally say "yes," to connecting with God is easy for me. It is especially easy when I am in church.

Has there ever been a time when you were sitting in church listening to the preacher, and everything that he or she was saying seemingly was directed toward you?

There were times at Wellspring when I have been listening to the preacher, and it seemed like he was talking directly to me. It is especially true of our preacher because he is so transparent. He says what he means and shares a lot.

That makes me feel good because I know that I am not the only one who has problems or the only one who is going through some challenges. I think that is a blessing.

It is also a gift from God. How can someone that you have never talked to about your problems, pretty much say what's on your mind and how you feel?

That's what saying "Yes," feels like to me; like God is giving me personal attention to help me get through this life.

SELF EXPLORATION: Please answer honestly and thoughtfully.

1. Do you ever feel like the writer, that God is using people to speak to you and encourage you? Describe a time this has happened?

_____

_____

_____

_____

_____

_____

_____

_____

_____

_____

_____
_____
_____
_____
_____
_____
_____
_____
_____

2. Did this experience strengthen your
   belief in God? Explain why it would
   or would not.

_____
_____
_____
_____
_____
_____
_____
_____
_____
_____
_____
_____

_____

_____

_____

_____

_____

_____

_____

Scriptures for further study:
<u>**God sending help**</u>**: Psalm 91:11,**
Genesis 19:151

Essay Two

Control has always been a big issue for me. I am a "take charge" person, and some say I can be like a steam roller. When I see something that I want or think that I need, I simply make it happen.

Working hard comes naturally to me, but I am learning that if your hard work is not aligned with God's purposes it can be in vain. We can sometimes work much harder because we do not trust God and have not allowed him to guide us. I struggle with letting God control situations because I don't feel completely comfortable giving up control. Allowing God to control situations sometimes can make me nervous, impatient, and frustrated.

Recently though, I truly accepted God into my life and although I still struggle with control sometimes, I get through it. I've seen the outcome of both ways of acting and accepting God instead of fighting God is the path that I want to travel.

By letting God take the reins, things come easier at times, my stress level has gone down and I enjoy my life more than I have before. God has given me the ability to truly see the good in life again.

SELF EXPLORATION: Please answer honestly and thoughtfully.

1. Do you remember a time when you felt heavily burdened by a decision that you had to make or an assignment that you needed to complete? How did you feel? Did you seek help or support? Was it

easier to move forward after
receiving input, help or guidance?

_____

_____

_____

_____

_____

_____

_____

_____

_____

_____

_____

_____

_____

_____

_____

_____

_____

_____

Essays on What Really Has Changed?

Essay One

I was once told by a pastor that I am a child of God and that God is working on me. I was always taught that in order to be saved, you had to get the Holy Ghost or speak in tongues and I was never that person.

Joining "Yes to God" has taught me that those things are not necessarily true. I do not have to go to church every Sunday, I can still listen to Rap and Rhythm and Blues music. I can still have a drink of wine sometimes and I can wear what I want.

Being saved has nothing to do with those things. God doesn't care about that. He cares about your relationship with him and the work He put you on this earth to do. All of the rest eventually takes care of itself if you follow Him. That freed me from trying to be

44

a person that I never thought I could be for God.

I know what God needs me to do for Him. I am a leader and I lead by example. I know now that all things can be done by and through Christ. I have no more shame in who I am. I am not scared of going to church, and I'm not scared to fall on the floor and praise and worship God.

Yes to God has taught me who God is. It has taught me how to hear from God and communicate with God. It has taught me how to walk by the Word of God, and to stick by God's side.

SELF EXPLORATION: Please answer honestly and thoughtfully.

1. In what environments do you feel most comfortable and why? Do you think that you can feel this way in church? What can you and others do to make church a place where people feel welcome and comfortable?

_____

_____

_____

_____

_____

_____

_____

_____

_____

_____

_____

_____

_____

_____

_____

_____

Scriptures for further study:
Romans 16:17-18, Romans 2:1-3

Essay Two

Absolutely everything has changed about me since I started attending church, starting with my personality to the choices I make on a day-to-day basis.

Ever since I began giving time to Wellspring and to the "Yes to God" group, I have evolved into the deeper side of myself and discovered who I really am inside of the shell I normally put myself in. I have found it easier to open up to others that I don't know, but before I would find it difficult and sometimes I would be very rigid when even just saying "hello" to people I didn't know.

Members of Wellspring as well as YTG have given me the love, loyalty and liability needed to freely express myself in order to grow a stronger relationship with God; especially through dancing and socializing with others my age, to gain relationships and understanding of common situations.

Being able to witness my own growth as a result of my involvement with the church and the group delights me, but hearing others tell me that they see me blossoming, tops it all off.

Personally, I have prayed more than I ever did, and I now realize that as long as I pray and keep faith in God, everything that's meant to be will be in line with God's will. In addition, I also find myself not giving up as easily in my relationships, especially the one with my long-time boyfriend. Our relationship has been put to the test multiple times, but when I find myself praying about it, things get better and I don't feel like giving up.

I am very pleased with the young woman that I am beginning to become and I feel so blessed to have such wonderful and beautiful people in my life to help me make and notice the transition in my life. I know I am not perfect and never will be and I have so much more spiritual growing to do, but I don't mind because I adore the journey. I look forward to many more experiences over the years to come.

Just as I had expressed to Ms. Nina before, I wouldn't ask to be a member of any other church or college-age group, because Wellspring and the "Yes to God" group have set a bar that none can reach.

SELF EXPLORATION: Please answer honestly and thoughtfully.

1. What changes would you like to see in yourself? Have you tried praying to God and asking for help? If not, do so and keep a notebook of successes and positive progress.

_____

_____

_____

_____

_____

_____

_____

_____

_____

_____

_____

_____

_____

_____

_____

_____

_____

_____

<u>Essay Three</u>

"Yes to God" has changed me a lot and in many ways. I attend church more often, I am learning more about God and I now understand that God is the biggest thing in my life.

I also have grown as a young man and a son of God. With the help that I am getting these days, there is no telling what great plans God has for me.

"Yes to God" is one of the biggest challenges I have had in my life, but I can honestly say that the group has supported me and is a gift from God.

If I wasn't involved with the "Yes to God" group, there is no telling what I would be doing, so I thank God for it. I appreciate the group and I am just thankful that it is there, and that it is making me a better person than I ever was.

SELF EXPLORATION: Please answer honestly and thoughtfully.

1. Do you believe that a relationship with God can really improve your life by helping you become more than you thought you were equipped to become? Have you ever prayed and asked God to show you what he wanted you to do?

_____

_____

_____

_____

_____

_____

_____

_____

_____

_____

_____

_____

_____

_____

_____

_____

_____

2. Do you think that being around
   others who want to improve their
   lives in this way, might be helpful?
   Why or Why not?

_____

_____

Don't stop here. Begin to keep a journal of your thoughts, ideas, and responses to things that happen or that you witness. When you think God has spoken to you, shown you something or sent someone else to tell you something, write it down in your journal with a date.

Later, this will help you to remember God's existence and activity in your life and signs of his personal relationship with you.

Have discussions with your friends about some of the issues brought forth in these essays. As a result, you may choose to come together to explore and discover just what God has planned for your life.

About the Writers

God gifted the idea for this book to Nina Thompson. Ms. Thompson established the college-aged ministry "Yes to God" in June 2013 and serves as its minister, as well as Wellspring's Church Administrator. With the help and support of Ms. Zita Casey, who provides much-needed prayer and spiritual input and Mrs. Valarie Williams, who provides the physical nourishment during our meetings, the group has thrived and matured in Christ since its inception.

The contributors are members of this ministry team, which is supported by the Missouri Annual Conference of the United Methodist Church, under the direction and guidance of Rev. Dr. F. Willis Johnson, Jr. and the family of Wellspring Church in Ferguson, Missouri.

They are extremely thankful to their fearless pastor and wonderful "church" family for the encouragement and support.

"Yes to God" Members

- ✓ Taylor Banks
- ✓ Cameron Emanuel
- ✓ Merilyn Gibson
- ✓ Brandon Hart
- ✓ Willie Little, Jr.
- ✓ Charisse Moore
- ✓ Kelly Mueller
- ✓ Adrina Phillips
- ✓ Akyiah Phillips
- ✓ Elizabeth Randle
- ✓ Anisah Williams

"Yes to God" College-Age Ministry

Wellspring Church

33 S. Florissant Road

Ferguson, MO 63135

www.wellspringchurchstl.org

Contact: Nina Thompson, 314-521-4217/

314-550-2004

For discounted bulk orders of this book or Ms. Thompson's other book, "Church Hurt Ain't No Joke," please contact Nina Thompson at 314-550-2004 or www.nicheprandcomm@sbcglobal.net

www.ingramcontent.com/pod-product-compliance
Lightning Source LLC
Chambersburg PA
CBHW061754040426
42447CB00011B/2294